BEST PRACTICES OF ACADEMIC LIBRARY INFORMATION TECHNOLOGY DIRECTORS – A report from Primary Research Group

2

ISBN #:1-57440-072-X

TABLE OF CONTENTS

4

SUMMARY OF MAIN FINDINGS

ELECTRONIC RESERVES

For most colleges surveyed, more than 50% of course reserve materials are online. PDF's for download is the preferred format but url based selections are becoming more common. Australia's Monash University has reached licensing agreements with publishers for electronic course reserves that are similar to the Copyright Clearinghouse regime in the USA

IN-LIBRARY PRINTING FOR STUDENTS

Most libraries have moved away aggressively from offering free printing to students.

Most libraries have plans on the shelf to digitize their special collections. However, the lack of consensus on ways to proceed has led some to postpone these decisions or to reduce their scope. Unlike in public libraries, where demand is being stimulated by the public, demand for digitization of academic library collections is still mostly "top down."

TECHNOLOGY CENTERS

Technology Centers in academic libraries, often initially conceived for faculty or specialized students in art or engineering, are increasingly used by the average student. Supply, properly marketed and conveniently situated, stimulates demand, surprisingly broad based demand.

USE OF LAPTOPS

This is an area that calls out for much more study and research. Slowly, students are becoming accustomed to bringing their laptops into the library, and even preferring to use their own computers to those supplied by the library.

LENDING OUT LAP TOPS IN THE LIBRARY

In general, students appear to appreciate the option, of borrowing laptops from their library, and most libraries that offer this service report high levels of student enthusiasm. In addition, libraries report virtually no problems with theft or even poor maintenance of equipment. However, the time demands of storing, distributing, maintaining, providing net access, and assuring compliance with legally mandated use provisions leads many librarians to seek to limit the programs. In addition, the availability of lap tops in the library does not appear to significantly affect use of other library workstations.

USE OF PHP PROGRAMMING

One participant points out that many cutting edge library services require php programming and that many smaller libraries in particular focus excessively on workstation maintenance and other issues.

DEVELOPMENT OF URL RESOLVERS

Problems remain, particularly with the integration of small publishers into the standard URL resolvers. Most libraries have purchased off the shelf software and prices have come down for reliable URL systems. In time, URL resolvers will become standard equipment for all academic libraries, as they now are for research libraries. End user enthusiasm for faster and more comprehensive URL resolvers will foster greater compatibility and all publishers are slowly but steadily adjusting to their ubiquity and influence.

USE OF EBOOKS

Ebook usage is steadily increasing especially among smaller libraries. Increased ease of use for patrons and librarians, a focus on downloadable titles rather than special viewing devices, and an increase in the number of titles available, has led to an upsurge in demand and usage. Other factors that have stimulated Ebook usage are the continuing advance of distance and cyberlearning, and the better integration of Ebooks into course management and electronic reserve systems and library catalogs. Some users complain about incompatibility among different vendors of Ebooks.

AUTOMATION OF ELECTRONIC COLLECTION MANAGEMENT

There is some interest in specialized software that automates the management of electronic assets in collections, providing copyright proviso's, usage restrictions, payment terms, renewal notices, changes in contract terms, and other facets of electronic collection management. Nonetheless, most librarians view existing commercial software for such functions as overpriced or unnecessary and many libraries have home grown systems that function reasonably effectively.

THE IMPORTANCE OF MARKETING NEW TECHNOLOGIES

The librarians in the study emphasize the importance of outreach to patrons. Technology does not market itself. Students need to be trained in how to use the technologies and where to find them. If the librarians seek the students out, position equipment where it will get maximum exposure, then students will not only use the equipment (or software) but find ways to use them previously not anticipated by the librarians. Ease of use, convenience, physical proximity and end user education are all important issues in maximizing the effectiveness of library technology. It seems like a platitude, but the importance of basic marketing is easily forgotten, and marketing well is often the difference between making an investment work or rendering it underutilized.

DIGITZATION OF SPECIAL COLLECTIONS

Most libraries have some kind of wish list for the digitization for their special collections, particularly their photographic collections. However, expertise is still limited and plans are thin for integrating digitized special collections into library catalogs, or publicizing them effectively over the web. More thought needs to be given to the integration of special collections in to mainstream library catalogs and how to publicize special collection over the web, or in partnership with other institutions. Also, databases gain force when they are combined with other databases and form a kind of convenient shopping center around particular themes such as: "the Civil War" (rather than "The Civil War in Southwestern Alabama"), or "Flowers and Fauna of the American West" (rather than "Flowers of Western Nebraska") or "Canadian Urban Architecture 1900-19." rather than "Public Buildings of Manitoba, 1900-1950. Databases that are combined can be marketed to specialized scholars, industry and the general public but it is much more difficult to market the highly specialized databases that universities tend to develop from their special collections.

WIRELESS ACCESS

As might be expected wireless access is accelerating quickly. However, in general, use of wireless is far higher by business students, especially graduate business students, than other groups.

Dell appears to have taken over much of the new workstation market; proponents often cite the ease of maintenance rather than system capabilities as a major factor in their purchase. The distinction between library maintained workstations and those maintained in the Library by the college IT department or other entities has faded over time, and in five years all general access library workstations may be more or less similar. Most librarians still believe that they spend too much time on workstation maintenance.

VIRTUAL REFERENCE SERVICES

In general, their influence in the academic library world has not been as great as among public libraries. Most of the larger libraries have a service through a major vendor but most of the smaller libraries have either home grown systems or nothing at all.

UNIFIED SEARCH INTERFACE

Thus far, much is being written about a search interface that would ideally connect all library assets – cataloged and previously uncataloged and all internet resources – into a vast universe that could be searched from a single interface. Many libraries are studying this issue but few feel the need to make any dramatic moves in this direction. Off the shelf and home grown software that helps libraries to unify special collections or integrate them into main collections should become more popular in academic libraries in the near future.

PC MAINTENANCE

Academic library technical staffs appear less knowledgeable than their counterparts in public libraries over the issue of image updating of personal computers and workstations. The time demands of image updating are still a very central and implacable problem for academic library technologists who spend an inordinate amount of time on the issue.

LEWIS & CLARK COLLEGE

Lewis & Clark College is a private college located in Portland, Oregon that has an FTE enrollment of approximately 3,000. The College has a law school and various masters programs, but its focus is mostly on undergraduate education. The law school has a separate library; otherwise all library services are centralized. We spoke with Mr. Mark Dahl, Assistant Director for Systems and Access Services.

TECHNOLOGY STAFF AND BUDGET

The library has a small technology budget (apart from salaries) of about $30,000 per year; about half of which is spent on software for the integrated library system, as well as *Dreamweaver*, *Photoshop* and other applications: the College Administration also pays for some types of application software under general college-wide licenses. The Library technology staff has 1.5 FTE positions, including the director, and one student helper per term.

ELECTRONIC RESERVES

The library scans information for library reserve using adobe acrobat and an Apache web server; the PDF's are available over the internet for download and are cataloged in the library's ILS. The library keeps print copies on reserve for students who prefer materials in paper formats. The scanning itself is done by the circulation department, not the IT department. The circulation department is open 24 hours a day, the result of a peculiar demand from the student council, and much such scanning is done at night,

PRINTING TECHNOLOGY

Students can print 250 pages per semester free of charge. All printing beyond this level costs 6 cents per page.

VIRTUAL REFERENCE SERVICES:

The Library uses a virtual reference chat service based on a well- known customer service software called PHP LIVE. This software is not specifically designed for libraries but Dahl believes it is just as effective as those that are and its low cost - $250.00 per year –also makes it attractive. The software is published by Osi Codes. "It doesn't have co-browsing," notes Dahl, "but it is enough to establish a dialog with a patron that works. We have had it for about a year and a half."

UR RESOLVER

Dahl developed the library's Url Resolver and wrote about the effort in the February 2004 Edition of *Computers in Libraries* Magazine. "We have a database that has our print and electronic journal holdings, and this just checks them against that database and returns links to the sources. If you are in a research database, an abstract comes up; if the full text is not available right there you can click on this button that says GET ITEM. It will check all of our electronic and print access and it will tell you if we have it electronically. It will then give you a link that will take you to the article, sometimes directly and sometimes you have to do a little search. It depends on how integrated the journal provider is with open URL.

"It did not take us that long (to develop the system). I worked on it for a couple of weeks in 2003 and then spent a few more weeks in the next year - and it has required periodic updates."

Dahl says that off the shelf software is not more widely available, but that some colleges still do it themselves. Williamette University, a college in the Portland area, also developed its own URL resolver, says Dahl, who also recommends an off the shelf solution.

"You can get a pretty good resolver from Serial Solutions - their article linker is pretty moderately priced and it is a good product," he says.

TECHNOLOGY INVESTMENT

Dahl says that in the near future the Library would like to invest "in developing its digital collections a little bit more. We would like to buy a digital collection management system like Content DM and we also might invest in a federated search system; it is a piece of software that allows you to search multiple databases at once. There are some open source options there as well."

LIBRARY AND INSTRUCTIONAL TECHNOLOGY CENTER

The Library is developing a special classroom in which to teach library technology skills. Dahl describes the effort: "We are putting in an instructor workstation and a fixed projector; then there will be wireless laptops that can be passed around. It (reliance on wireless computing) will make the space pretty versatile; it can be used when everyone needs a computer and situations when only the instructor is needed. We are going to do some capital equipment requests to get some furniture and computer equipment budget."

WIRELESS

"The university has a wireless network. We were one on the first areas on campus to get wireless access," says Dahl. Dahl likes the wireless option but sometimes feels it puts heavy demands on this modest tech support staff. He notes that: "Sometimes we have to do more tech support on laptop computers to configure them for wireless access, and the computers must have a special application on them that they are up to date and have virus protection. Getting that to work is kind of a challenge sometimes."

WORKSTATIONS

The library offers for patron access 25 workstations that it maintains and 50 others that the College IT department maintains. The workstations maintained by the IT Department have traditionally offered applications software and internet access while the workstations maintained by the library have offered access to the catalog and databases. However, now that virtually all databases have migrated to the web, and library management decided to offer applications software on the workstations it maintains, the distinction between the two types of workstations has faded. Nonetheless, Dahl points out that it is still sometimes useful for the Library to actually control some of the workstations in the institutional sense. He notes that: "We can tweak them the way we want to. We have our own special screen savers that advertise services of the library - there are some advantages to doing it ourselves. At some point we would like to integrate the two -- it is kind of an administrative hurdle."

WEB SITE

Dahl is more involved in web site management than the IT directors at larger colleges. "I am the central person for maintaining it. (The law library has its own web developer/webmaster) and I share that responsibility with one of the reference librarians. The (5) reference librarians maintain all their own subject pages Maintaining the web site accounts for a third of my time -- if you count all the different applications that are running."

At any one time the Library has 10-15 PHP applications running form its web site, including an interlibrary loan form, a script that allows you to browse the audio visual collection, a search engine for the site and other applications.

Although running the web site and the web server "is quite a bit of work," Dahl thinks it is well worth it, adding: "We can do a lot of things that libraries that don't have their own web server can't do. When you run your own proxy server -- that is the most important thing -- you can build local database driven pages like the audio reserve system, do a customized open URL resolver, or set up system to manage the content on your pages. We could just use the campus web server for free. Our server costs $4500 but the Linux software just costs 50 bucks per year. The base maintenance to keep the system going is an hour or two per week but then there is all the tweaks on all the different applications. Perhaps I would not have a server if I had someone at the IT department that I worked with real closely but I have never heard that happening on a college campus. When a whole campus is dependent on a web server you do not want to spend too much time on library applications (if you are a college IT Department director)."

ADVICE TO OTHER LIBRARIES

According to Dahl, "Smaller libraries often suffer because they do not have expertise in PHP programming. "It pays off to get some staff that can do web applications. That is how you are able to deliver strong, cutting edge services in libraries; it is not in local area networks, or in workstations, or in CD-ROM's, it is web applications. Libraries need to build that expertise. Too many smaller libraries -- if they have a systems person -- all that person works on is the integrated library system or in setting up pc's. But they need to work on web applications and that is how they will be able to provide what people want. Cooperation with the IT department can help but the problem with the IT departments is that they have so much infrastructure demand on them that they do not have the time to put into library and educational technologies. They can't focus on providing customized educational technologies."

THE RESEARCH LIBRARIES GROUP

DESCRIPTION OF THE RESEARCH LIBRARIES GROUP

The Research Libraries Group (RLG) is a non-profit corporation initially founded in the 1970's by the research libraries of Harvard, Columbia, Yale and the New York Public Library. The RLG now has 160 member institutions worldwide, of which 114 are in North America and 44 in Europe. Virtually all are major research libraries and most are also academic libraries through the RLG membership roster also includes major museums and archives. The RLG bases its membership fees on the size of the member library's overall budget. The RLG is essentially a cooperative organization controlled by its members who contribute resources to solve problems of mutual interest that are most efficiently confronted through joint efforts. RLG members thus enjoy the economies of scale associated with joint efforts, and also are able to gain leverage in influencing efforts that require the adoption of standards accepted by a range of institutions. The RLG's efforts have tended to have the greatest impact in those areas of the most volatile technological ferment for libraries. We spoke with Mr. Jim Michalko, CEO of the RLG, and asked him about the most pressing and important technological challenges facing research libraries over the next few years.

THE PRESERVATION OF DIGITAL MATERIALS

As more and more personal and professional communications have shifted to the web, the preservation of web-based materials of scholarly interest has become a major pre-occupation of the scholarly community. For example, much of the history of the 2004 presidential campaign is in the web-based campaigns of the major candidates. Long standing scholarly vehicles exist for the preservation of broadcast news, print ads, op-ed pieces, newspaper, magazine and broadcast commentary. However, web sites appear and disappear, and no reliable vehicle exists to assure access future scholarly access to important web sites, newsgroups and other cyberspace information resources. The problem will grow worse and worse since -- in 20 years -- scholars looking at the early years of the 21'st century -- may find that many of the most pertinent resources will have vanished. Explains Michalko: "Libraries and archives and museums have always collected gray literature, things that are not published but you might want it for historical purposes -- say all of the communications of the Solidarity movement in Poland. What is the equivalent of that in the digital world? What does it mean to keep and house and make permanently available these kinds of web sites?"

"Only a certain category of institution really has the capability of managing a repository. We will need third parties. It will probably result in a certification effort so that third party providers are going to have to have certain kinds of characteristics."

In addition to the digitization of the every day "stuff" of history, scholarship and the "scholarly trail", the notes, the communication, the "letters" of "men of letters" has all become digital grist.

"There are pre-prints in almost all academic disciplines," says Michalko, "all of that kind of stuff has been the purview of libraries and now that is all in digital form. They (librarians) have to capture it, keep it. It is not instead of it is in addition to what they are (already) doing. There has been a huge shift in the academic environment."

Michalko believes that the technological challenges involved in preserving digital resources for scholarship are the least of the challenges involved.

"It is fraught," he says, "and it goes way beyond the technology challenge; it has policy and legal implications and has some really interesting access challenges associated with it. It is going to rebound all over the information and research landscape and it is now starting to resonate with a lot of people."

"There are both copyright and contract law challenges associated with this stuff. In the print world we had our practices established and honed over many many years. Now we have to ask: Is the material there? Can I use it? What are the rules associated with it? One can imagine 25 years from now the entire face of scholarship having a completely different complexion."

A problem related to that of preserving the vast amounts of materials in digital format that are of potential scholarly use is: how do libraries provide finding aids or in some way catalog these resources so that they are as accessible as books and journals? According to Michalko, academic and research libraries are just starting to grapple with this issue.

A third, and indeed related issues, is: how do libraries cope with the vast alternative world of information accessed through Google and other search engines? Libraries can condescend to search engines and the quality of information on the web, but the reality is simply that a new generation of students has been raised on search engines.

"The fact is we are just about having our first generation who believes that everything that you need to know is on the web and whose paradigm for information seeking has been formed by the search engine," says Michalko in a matter of fact tone, "How will this affect information searching and critical thinking? We have to start looking at these organizations as partners rather than problems. The recent announcement and appearance of the Google Scholar data service was a really interesting example of the search engines realizing that there are some specialized communities out there that require special approaches. I applaud them - it is an early example of a new and different type of partnership. We (research and academic libraries) have to think about questions such as: how do cultural institutions make themselves present in the new information environment? And what is the nature and form of the partnership between academia and those who provide access to the web right now?"

HOW CLOSE TO THE SEARCH ENGINES IS TOO CLOSE?

The libraries need the search engines and the search engines need the libraries. Libraries are incomplete without access to the world of the search engines but the search engines are incomplete without access to the world of the libraries. If mutual need is so great why is cooperation so difficult? One reason is that the search engines are governed by the internet credo of "available to all on demand" while the libraries are governed by the principle "available to the affiliated when available." Library patrons are demanding libraries to behave more like the web, but web surfers want a more library-like internet. Web surfers want more high value content (like libraries) and library searchers want click on demand delivery and worldwide resource searching at the click of a mouse.

The problem is: when libraries index their resources on the web, what happens if they get requests from those who are not entitled to access to their collections? According to Michalko, the research libraries have for the most part already confronted and conquered this reaction.

"Early on they said: I could not deal with that (attention from non-traditional mass users) but these attitudes have changed since. Your visibility on the web says something about your institution's influence, visibility, etc. It is something that they now have begun to value. Museums used to think: if you can find my stuff on the web then you won't come to visit the museum but now they know the opposite is true The search engine is discovering for them this additional world of information and they are wondering about how to incorporate it. The traditional providers (libraries, museums, archives, etc) have come to terms with the fact that they need to be present in the new discovery channels. They need to see themselves reflected there."

A BOOK IS A BOOK IS A BOOK

Libraries have represented their inventory in catalogs fundamentally as lists of things but web sites such as Amazon present their inventory in dynamic ways, presenting a work's cover, its sales rank in the inventory, information about a book's author and even about its readers, such as what other books its readers prefer. The dynamic web sites present the cataloged items in ways calculated both to entice and allow the potential end user to "size up" the item. Michalko warns that libraries must take note of this as an advance, and not condescend or poke fun.

"The way that they describe what they own has been optimized for physical items in a physical inventory and it has served the world of scholarship well for hundreds of years. But how should I describe a physical item so that it is useful in a web environment? A lot of practices that might be optimized for the physical inventory will change. How will I optimize this so that it is most useful on the web? The paradigm is Amazon. I looked at kids trying to find something in a library catalog and they were wondering why it did not have a picture of the cover. Bringing the world of print into the discovery channels. I think is a really important step that they (research and academic libraries) are now entertaining."

FORMAL RELATIONS BETWEEN THE WORLD OF SCHOLARSHIP AND THE SEARCH ENGINES

Cooperation between the two worlds of information searching may take a formal or informal form. The RLG has large centralized depositories of data and it has been having discussions with major search engines about incorporating aspects of its databases into the search engines indices. However, not all cooperation will come about as a result of specific agreements.

"What we have to think about is the range of materials and the historical accumulation of materials. We have to make that stuff present. So it is those kinds of challenges that we are grappling with now. It does not necessarily mean that you will have explicit agreements between the two sectors, it will be acknowledgement to take best advantage of one another."

SEARCHING AND TRANSLATION

One of the largest obstacles to truly unified searching - the capacity to search enormous databases of information on the web, in library catalogs and depositories, and elsewhere -- is language, old fashioned language -- Japanese, English, Italian, French, and Swahili. Michalko envisions a search engine solution that would be able to search "foreign language" collections and return results that are comprehensible to an English language searcher. This does not necessarily mean direct translation but enough translation capability so that obvious references in other languages could me made available in searches.

"We ought to be able to search in our own language and discover what it relevant even if it is in another language. We are gong to need some technological leap -- not necessarily translation -- but it is a problem for research and for the academy more generally."

ENHANCED IMAGE SEARCHING AND PRESENTATION

Another significant problem that needs to be tackled, says Michalko, is the relatively rudimentary state of searching for images on the web.

"What if we could put3D images of stuff in museums out on the web? What does it mean to encounter a 3D object in that web space? How close can you come to replacing the physical experience? I remember going back. We borrowed some objects from museums -- Greek urns -- and we showed them in 3D imaging and the first question from someone in the back of the room was: Can I see the bottom of the pot? Apparently it was very critical for research purposes to see the bottom of the pot. When you have lots of objects out here -- how do you search for it and how do you present them? We have not ratcheted up our ability to search images at all. It is still all text driven. When we have large depositories of images -- how can we search them in useful and meaningful ways for academic and research purposes?"

"On the whole, museums are not nearly as concerned as they once were over making their collections available on the web. One concern that they no longer have is that someone else would seize their images, reproduce them as bootleg copies, and sell them. This has not really happened, and museums themselves have not made a lot of money in peddling images of their collections. Consequently, they are much more likely to view the images as teases to flirt with their potential audience on the web, hoping to seduce them into the museum themselves. It is a strategy that has worked for many."

"Their success is partially defined by their success in displaying their items on the web," says Michalko, "and that is a welcome change - they are committed to the digital world."

Smaller museums in particular need help in making their collections web-accessible. "Once you get just below the brand names but they do not have the kind of staff and onsite intelligence to take the best advantage and they are looking for third parties to cooperate with - they don't have the internal resources to do this. Maybe this is just a by-product of where the cycle is right now. If things (production tools) get standardized and then institutions that are a little less well off - -they will do better."

RED LIGHT/GREEN LIGHT

The RLG has tried to explore some of the themes it is speculating about in a new product that it is developing, a website dubbed REDLIGHTGREEN.ORG (.com and .net work equally well). The site - use of which is available free of charge to all with a web browser -- catalogs the availability of more than 32 million books.

"We actually took all of the books that we know about -- 32 million unique titles -- and we built a web site that we put out for free. We want people who are interested to use it --Just type in some words. Try it," he suggests.

WWW.REDLIGHTGREEN.COM///

The site will give you references to the more than 500 editions of Gulliver's Travels or include Spanish language reference to Don Quixote. It will also locate an online version of it, if one is available. In addition, the site has links to information about authors.

"We did do some computational linguistics. We know it works. You can search for things using Search in Spanish and then you will get stuff in those languages but results from other languages will get bubbled into your results."

Initially, RLG beta tested the site to students at NYU, the University of Minnesota and Princeton. The site is aimed at students, but ultimately RLG wants to calibrate the site so that it could be used by scholars and researchers as well, who often need access to more arcane materials than do students.

"Ultimately what you would like to be able to do is to say: "I am an Expert" and you would present the results in one way, or say: "I am just Starting" and you would get another set of results. Pick some topic that you know about -- if this thing is working right you ought to look at the first screen and say to yourself: I know most of that stuff - if there are a few things."

UNIVERSITY OF TEXAS AT ARLINGTON

GENERAL DESCRIPTION OF UT ARLINGTON

The University of Texas At Arlington has approximately 25,200 FTE students; 25% of whom are in graduate and professional programs. Approximately 2,000 more are in a continuing education program; the rest, in the main undergraduate degree programs. UT Arlington is a Class One Level Institution, one of four in Texas, along with UT at El Paso, San Antonio, Dallas and Arlington (UT Austin is the flagship research institution). We spoke with Mr. Gerald Saxon, Dean of Libraries at the University of Texas, Arlington.

The library has six separate locations; three full libraries and three locations that offer access to electronic resources in a library-type setting. Five of the libraries/electronic info centers are dispersed throughout the campus while one is in neighboring Fort Worth where the University "is trying to attract students so that they don't have to drive to Arlington," notes Saxon.

WORKSTATIONS

The Library provides a cumulative total of 225 public access workstations in the six buildings or centers, of which roughly 75% are in the main library, 15% in a science and engineering library, and about 10% dispersed in the other libraries and info centers, including 4 in Fort Worth.

The electronic information centers are relatively small, averaging about 400 square feet, but provide an important tentacle for the library, enabling it to reach into necessary nooks and crannies in pursuit of a mobile and demanding student body.

ROLE OF WIRELESS

All of the University's libraries are wireless enabled, although wireless usage seems most intensive in the business library. The main library checks out laptops to patrons for two defined time periods, overnight or, for those laptops that circulate inside the library's structures, for three hours with the possibility of one three hour renewal..

"The library has a total of 50 laptops and they are out all the time," comments Saxon, "and it has been interesting. We have been checking out laptops for 2.5 years and we have only lost one due to theft -- a student went to the bathroom and left it out and it was stolen. And only 2 have been damaged." Despite this fine record, Saxon warns that the time demands of laptop maintenance can be daunting for a time pressed library staff. Says Saxon: "they have to be recharged, cleaned, and you must make sure that the

30

software is up to date. Students must agree to certain things; they have to agree to pay for its replacement (if they do not return it) and they must agree to abide by the state laws regarding the internet, and (assuring compliance) with this all takes time. We have carts to which they must be plugged into and these carts have to be maintained. As a matter of fact we feel we are at the top of what we can accommodate."

In addition, since laptop technology tends to develop and change quickly, laptops are on a two year replacement cycle, while all other computers in the library are on a three year cycle.

Initially, the students themselves paid for the laptops through their technology fees; one year the student congress decided to use the fees to acquire the laptops for the library. However, this is not necessarily a grant that will be repeated. Initially, the library purchased Gateways but switched to Dell after deciding that Dell's customer service was superior. The laptops are loaded with Microsoft Office, software for OPAC access and access to University domains.

ELECTRONIC OUTREACH

The Library offers three "electronic services" information centers that tend to be relatively small rooms – about 400 square feet on average – staffed by a librarian or library assistant – and offering 4-6 workstations. One is located in the College's School of Social Work, and another in neighboring Fort Worth.

The Electronic Services centers do not offer print books or periodicals. Nonetheless, they are often jammed with students and Saxon credits them with a rebound in library attendance. "A lot of our students do not live in dorms and they have breaks in their schedule in the day (but don't have the inclination or convenience to go home) and the centers are a convenient place for students to study, work and socialize. The centers also offer free printing, though the Library may introduce a metered printing service in the near future," explains Saxon.

"We have noticed that our library gate counts have gone up. We get 65,000 people coming into a library facility weekly. Our statistics have gone up (unlike many other academic research libraries)."

LIBRARY IT DEPARTMENT STAFF

The Libraries IT department has a staff of six people FTE; they focus on servers and software, and connectivity issues. The Library also has a Digital Libraries Services Staff that focuses more on the website, licensing and databases and other electronic content oriented issues. The Digital Libraries Staff has a staff of 10 FTE. The head of Digital Libraries, and the assistant head, are librarians; three others are educational designers and web designers, while five are library assistants with "great technical skills." Notes Saxon. In addition the Library has an Information Resources staff of fourteen which deals almost exclusively with acquisitions and content issues.

HELP DESK

The Library help desk is actually staffed by the University's Office for Information Technology. The help desk actually serves students and staff throughout the University, but many of the help desk personnel actually work from the library. "We asked them to join us three and a half years ago," says Saxon, "as part of an effort to create a student friendly library environment. We put in a coffee bar and a work space for students and we asked the University Office for Information Technology for students" (to man a library located help desk).

DIGITAL MEDIA CLASSROOM

The Library has developed a multi media production center equipped with 16 computers, scanners, video editing equipment, flash software, video streaming software, DVD's and video players and digital cameras. Originally the production center was aimed largely at instructors, with the objective of helping them to integrate new technological and presentation tools into their teaching. However, the center's main clientele, to the surprise of Library management, has not been instructors, but students. "And not just film students," explains Saxon, but engineering and business students as well."

The Library opened the center in 2001, starting out with two modest workstations but quickly the number of workstations increased to 16 as demand grew. "It helped also to put it in a more visible location," said Saxon, since accessibility fosters experimentation. The center has three full time staff members who are on call to help patrons to the use the center's hardware and software. The Library initially used a grant to get started but now the center is supported directly in the Library budget.

DIGITAL LIBRARY SERVICES

The Library has promulgated several efforts to digitize its special collections. Perhaps its most significant digitization venture is an effort to digitize the Library's formidable map collection, largely relating to maps of the Gulf of Mexico and the American Southwest; some maps date to 1493.

The Library also has an Oral History Project with prominent Mexican Americans – dubbed *Tejano Voices*. The Library has digitized transcripts of the 75 oral histories and layered over audio of the interviews themselves

The Library is also undertaking the vast task of digitizing its historic photograph collection of more than 4 million photographs, a huge historic photograph archive that was once the photo repository of The *Fort Worth Star Telegram*. "The newspaper transferred all of the rights to reproduce and sell them," said Saxon, when we inquired about the Library's rights to use the collection.

INFORMATION LITERACY STAFF

The library has an information literacy staff of six people FTE but no formal information literacy requirement. The information literacy staff mostly instructs undergraduates while the graduate and professional school patron tutoring load is handled mostly by subject specific reference librarians.

ELECTRONIC COURSE RESERVES

Items on electronic course reserves account for about 70% to 75% of reserve requests from instructors, according to Saxon, who notes that "We pay all the copyright fees for the instructors. We want usually about three weeks (early warning from the instructors about what items they need) prior to the beginning of the semester. We ask for it but we do not ordinarily get it."

PRINTING TECHNOLOGY

Currently, the Library does not charge students for printing, but next year the Library is hoping to implement a system through which students will get some free printing, and then be charged for additional printing. The Library has already ordered the Pharos Print Management System and expects to implement it. In the past year, the Library spent

$170,000 for toner, printing and repairs and would like to recoup at least part of this outlay.

AUTOMATING ELECTRONC COLLECTIONS MANAGEMENT

The Library is currently looking into an automated collection management system. A staff member is currently trying to develop a home grown system, but the Library may also consider an off the shelf alternative.

ADVICE TO OTHER LIBRARIES

Make sure that you make a priority the availability of resources to update the library's software and hardware, as "it has taken a decade to move our replacement budget up," says Saxon. Also, "Make sure you have adequate staff to deal with all of the issues that are going to come up. Train them or pay for their training. Technology training is so expensive compared to other forms of library training."

THE UNIVERSITY OF WASHINGTON, SEATTLE

ABOUT THE LIBRARY

The University of Washington (Seattle) is a major research university with approximately 30,000 students FTE. We spoke with Mr. William Jordan, Associate Director of Libraries for Information Technology Services. The Library has more than 20 buildings, and all libraries on campus, except the law library, report to the main library and are considered functional organizational segments of the main library.

VIRTUAL REFERENCE SERVICES

The Library has been using *Questionpoint* for about two years. "We are pretty well committed to it as this point," says Jordan.

WIRELESS ACCESS

The business and health sciences libraries have wireless access, as do parts of the main library. We continue to try to expand access as funding allows," notes Jordan.

We asked what the impact of wireless access had been on physical attendance at the library. Jordan noted: "It makes you more productive when you are in the building but it does not affect actual usage of the library. We did not see a huge jump in the gate counts but it changes the way that you might use the library. So much work now meshes library materials with other materials. (with wireless) You can get your hands on a range of resources."

URL LINK RESOLVER

The Library uses a turnkey system from Innovative Interfaces, the *Web Bridge*, for which it was one of the early test sites. "We continue to work with them to make it work better," says Jordan. "Some of t it needs more flow control so you can make more finely grained decisions -- as you work through your various decisions. I might want to put up a direct article link if I have enough data but if I don't maybe then I want something else (another level of link). We did some usability testing and we found that putting everything up in the users face just leads to confusion. Keeping data updated is also an ongoing problem. There is still a lot of wiggle room in the standard. There is a lot of resource specific profiling that needs to be done to make it work right."

ELECTRONIC COURSE RESERVE SYSTEM

The Library uses *Eres* from Docutech. Says Jordan: "We have had it for three or four years. About half of all assigned materials are now available through it. There has been a huge growth in the past two or three years." The system largely makes PDF downloads available to students, but also sometimes provides links to electronic resources, when available.

BUDGET PRIORITIES

"I think desktop hardware is still an ongoing issue; like most places we have not fully funded that. Hardware re-fresh is the biggest ongoing pain. There is nothing particularly exciting about that. We are looking at open source digital library developments; we were involved with the D space federation."

DIGITAL INITIATIVES

"We have a digital initiatives group that is mostly involved in digitizing local content or putting together faculty collections.

We work closely with the digital initiatives folks. We look at it from the technical side and we have been involved in the Million Books Project. A lot of libraries are sending out non copyright stuff to have it digitized. I don't know if we are going to do a lot of that in-house. It makes sense to sub-contract that and so much depends on the grant funding you can get to support it. The IT group would not lead on that."

UPGRADING WORKSATIONS

The library system has a total of 550 staff workstations and 300 --350 public access workstations. In addition, the Library hosts several hundred that are run by the computing labs. The undergrad library alone has 300 public access workstations. "I have about 900 workstations that are on our budget that we are trying to keep upgraded. Every four or five years they are functionally obsolete. We would like to keep to a 4 year replacement cycle though it will be slower in actuality, about five years, I think. I try to buy a couple of hundred per year. Most of our workstations are Dell. We pretty much went to Dell in 2000. We were happy with the service and the reliability was very good from the first batch we took. They have an image stable configuration so with my small group and 950 workstation, we can only manage them by rolling out the same image to all of the workstations. They do not change the internal components on you from week to week; we have been very happy with them. The stuff is all modularized now. Everything is on the motherboard now."

PRINTING TECHNOLOGY

Public printing is provided through the campus photocopying group, which provides it on a cost recovery basis using Pharos Software. Print outs cost 10 cents per page, and the University does not provide a free allotment for students.

SEPARATE TECHNOLOGY BUDGET AND STAFF

The Library IT department has 10 full time employees distributed as follows: 4 librarians, 5 technical staff, and one help desk employee (who focuses on staff problems).

The IT department gets some earmarked funding from the University and also has a departmental budget. All positions are library funded and are not grant dependent.

In addition to its 10 full time employees, the Technology Department has 4 student assistants who work an average of 20 hours per week. They are all undergraduates who earn from $9.50 to $11.00 per hour and none are work study funded. "They install software on workstations, they plug in things, climb under desks, do desktop support, that sort of thing," says Jordan.

SPECIAL TECHNOLOGY-RELATED DISBURSEMENTS FROM THE UNVERSITY

The IT Department often benefits from special disbursements to fund equipment purchases, often amounting to $150,000 to $200,000. "There is not really a fixed, permanent equipment line -- it is one time money, says Jordan, "but we have gotten something each year. One year the University did not make any equipment money available and many departments across campus were unhappy with that. Now we have a student technology fee. You can apply to the student technology fee committee, which is run by students, and they have bought some workstations for us in the past. The fee is: $45.00 per quarter or about $135.00 per year and it is student controlled and disbursed."

UNIFIED SEARCH INTERFACE

"We have not done anything thus far with any metasearch products. We understand that some institutions deployed them and then pulled them back. There were varying degrees of satisfaction. In some cases they will eat up your seat licenses. We are continuing to monitor it."

WEB SITE

The IT Department handles coordination and the usability testing. However, a committee drawn from many units has oversite and dozens and dozens of people contribute content. Some of it goes with your position responsibilities. The subject librarians expected to put up a subject page and we provide tools and templates to help them to do that. We've got a system for extracting relevant records from the catalog and then building A to Z lists. It took about six or seven months - it was a pretty intensive effort. We had a bit of a learning curve. It wouldn't take very long now. We developed it in late 1997, early 1998."

FATE OF "MY LIBRARY" APPLICATIONS

"We mostly 'glue' applications together. We are not working on "my library' type stuff - we had gone that way in the late 1990's but shut that system down this last year. It wasn't really used too much and most of the usage was not really customized. They just took the defaults - I can give you a web page that gives you the defaults. Our health science library has done a lot with role-based toolkits which provide a selection of resources that are appropriate for particular roles. There is a student toolkit, a researcher toolkit and those seem to be more useful than the personalized customization option, or at least they are more heavily used. Also it would have to integrate with the campus portal environment."

VANDERBILT UNIVERSITY

GENERAL DESCRIPTION

Vanderbilt University is one of America's major research universities perhaps best known for its programs in law, education and pharmacology. We spoke with Marshall Breeding, Library Technology Officer for the Jane and Alexander Heard Library of Vanderbilt University.

VIRTUAL REFERENCE

The Library initially started using LSSI Virtual Reference but did not get as much use as anticipated and switched to Questionpoint about two years ago. Breeding says that this system is well used. The Library contributes about 4 to 8 hours of reference staff time per day in answering Questionpoint traffic. The Library plans to stay with Questionpoint and also may join a virtual reference consortium sponsored by the Association of Southeast Research Libraries. This Association had formed a virtual reference consortium about a year ago which Vanderbilt initially elected not to join.

DIGITAL INITIATIVES

The Library is currently in the midst of a major strategic planning overhaul, one aspect of which is its plan to digitize aspect of its special collections. The Library' has various digital initiatives underway but its main initiative is to digitize the Vanderbilt television news archive. The Archive encompasses broadcast United States national news from 1968 onward and includes extensive footage from the national news broadcasts of ABC, CBS, and NBC; the archive added CNN in 1995 and Fox News in 2004. In addition to national daily news broadcasts, the collection includes coverage of special events, such as major speeches, political conventions and significant news conferences, as well as complete 24 hour coverage for about a week or two of the events of 9/11.

The networks maintain copyright to the broadcasts but the index to them is available on the web. The digitization project supplements Vanderbilt's existing videotape loan service from the archive, requests for which can be initiated through the Vanderbilt library web site.

The Library recently launched a subscription service for K-12 educational institutions through which it provides streaming video access to the CNN portion of the collection. End users can view it through a streaming media player but cannot save it. "Our agreement with CNN requires that it (the streaming video footage) be at least three days old." Only CNN has granted Vanderbilt the rights to use its footage in this fashion with the proviso that, as Breeding explains: "The streaming service is exclusively for educational users." However, the Vanderbilt video lending service, based on the same collection, "is for commercial use and the general public as well as for educational purposes." Consequently, the Library will continue its videotape loan program even after it digitizes the complete national broadcast news archive. Copyright law protects the traditional video access method but does not give Vanderbilt rights to stream video from the major networks.

The Library has already digitized all of its CNN footage and has started on the rest of its collection. Overall, it is about two fifths of the way through the digitization process and has digitized broadcasts through 1980 (as well as all of the CNN broadcasts). The Library is currently digitizing about 100 broadcasts per day.

In order to digitize the video collection, Vanderbilt developed its own workstation solution; it funded this hardware/software project through a National Science Foundation (NSF) grant. The workstation is crafted by melding together various pre-existing software and hardware components; the Library also obtained local grants to produce a dozen such workstations from the template developed with the NSF grant. For the most part, Vanderbilt developers used commercially available software such as Moviemaker and combined them with locally written Pearl scripts.

Consequently, the Vanderbilt library will have considerable film digitization production capacity when the current project ends. "We may end up partnering with other institutions to expand our collection but we do not have specific plans in place," says Breeding, referring to how Vanderbilt might use this capacity.

The Library also has an ongoing project to digitize the library's photographic archives

WORKSTATIONS

The libraries have about 150 workstations for public access; all have standard web browsers and some have the Microsoft Office suite.

ORGANIZATION OF THE LIBRARY INFORMATION TECHNOLOGY SERVICES GROUP

The unit has 11 FTE employees, five of whom are librarians: the rest are non-librarian professional staff. The focus of the unit's responsibilities are maintaining all servers and repositories and dealing with network and shared printing environment issues. The Group does not use very much student help. The law, business and biomedical libraries each have separate information technology staffs.

URL RESOLVER

The Library uses SFX.

WIRELESS ACCESS

Graduate business students are required to have laptops and Breeding feels that by far the most important impact of wireless access has been in the Management Library, while in the general business library, also wireless enabled, the impact has been relatively modest.

LIBRARY STAFF TRAINING

"There is not a training program in great depth. We have a standing group called technology support coordinators; they get updates from the LTIS Group. They get a little bit more training than others. It is a group of about 20 and they form a liaison to other departments of the Library over technology issues." The support coordinators receive some ad hoc technology training. "It is designed to make sure there is someone in each library that is better versed in technology issues than others in that library; it is both a communications group and a group of technology helpers. It has mixed reviews – whether it does enough is a question but it does help."

STUDENT TECHNOLOGY TRAINING

Student information literacy training is not a required part of the curriculum.

One of our campus libraries have done quite a bit – Peabody Library – used to be called the education library."

CALIFORNIA INSTITUTE OF TECHNOLOGY

DESCRIPTION OF THE CALIFORNIA INSTITUTE OF TECHNOLOGY

The California Institute of Technology (CIT) is one of the premier scientific research institutions the United States which regularly ranks among the top five universities in the country in grant money received for scientific research projects. CIT has an FTE enrollment of approximately a thousand undergraduates and a thousand graduate students, as well as about 1000 post doctoral researchers and 300 regular faculty in engineering and applied science, geology & planetary science, chemistry, biology, humanities and social science, physics- mathematics and astronomy. We spoke with Eric Vandevelde, Director of Library Information Technology.

LIBRARY DIMENSIONS

The Library encompasses five buildings or parts of buildings and includes 2 main library buildings and 3 sectional libraries housed in part of buildings that also house other facilities. The campus is relatively small and no two library locations are more than about 200 yards from one another.

DIMENSIONS OF THE LIBRARY STAFF

The overall library staff is 43 professionals; an additional 20-30 student helpers work 5-10 hours per week. The IT Department has an FTE staff of six. Mr. Vendevelde has a PHD in computing and moved over to the Library from the Applied Math Department. Two IT Department staff primarily do customer support such as help desk functions, system configuration, and basic equipment maintenance. One system administrator focuses on network and server administration, while one applications programmer maintains all Linux systems and does PHP programming.

DEVLELOPMENT OF DEPOSITORIES

The University requires all graduating doctoral students, with some exceptions, to deposit their thesis in a Library maintained digital depository. The depository is part of the library's open access initiative. Since 2002, students have been required to submit their thesis to the depository in PDF or postscript format, from which it is made available, not just to the CalTech community, but to the general public. Some provisions exist for students who wish to restrict access. Vandevelde explains:

"Only a tiny number restrict a part of the thesis for a limited amount of time- if there is a patent pending or if they are working on a couple of papers or if they are in the process of peer review. In 2003 138 theses were submitted and 102 had unrestricted access and 23 were restricted in some way, nine were withheld and four were mixed, meaning that they only restricted a chapter or so."

It has been much harder to get the cooperation of faculty. Faculty submission to the depository is voluntary and "is an extremely low proportion of what is published by CalTech," says Vendevelde, "and most of the technical repositories are historical documents. It is actually older research. The only active depository to which faculty submit on a regular basis is in computer science. You have an ingrained culture of pre-prints in computer science. This culture does not exist at all in biology or medicine where they are very secretive until the point of publishing. Physicists are very open but they do it (open access) via Cornell."

DIGITAL INITIATIVES

The Library's efforts in the area have been relatively modest thus far.

"The only thing that is going on is oral histories of scientists," say Vandevelde, "Every faculty member is interviewed by the archive department; those interviews are transcribed and made available and the archive is digitizing all of them. The Geology Department has maps to digitize. It is definitely our ambition to go after these things, but now we are using these new media in a very conventional way. The demand (for digitization of special collections) really has not been there; it is us more trying to stimulate the demand rather than people coming to us."

UNIFIED SEARCH INTERFACE

The Library is actively working a solution so that all depositories can be searched from one place. "I have not been able to convince our librarians that we need a federated search engine. I would be interested in going in that direction."

TECHNOLOGY EDUCATION

The University has no formal information literacy requirement and the emphasis on post graduate education and research tends to create a larger universe than at other universities of individuals who are best served by subject specific librarians. The Library concentrates on informal meetings as well as lunch time seminars on general information literacy or on specific databases. The library also offers a popular seminar on how to put together your electronic thesis.

LENDING OUT OF LAPTOPS

The Library has been lending out lap tops inside the library since 1997. "We were one of the first to do it," says Vandevelde. "We keep a stock of 1 to lend out and they are mostly out at night (as opposed to during the day in the Library itself). In seven years we have had not a single theft; we had some damage in the early years,"

IMPACT OF WIRELESS ACCESS

Most of the libraries have a wireless capability. It has been gradually but not quite fully implemented. According to Vandevelde, the introduction of wireless "did not have as much of an effect on the head count as I had anticipated. We have seen a growth in people bringing their own laptops to the library but it is much less than I had anticipated. I had been making the argument that we should get out of the computer business and rely on people bringing their own computers. At some point (in the knowledge acquisition and usage process) going to a shared computer must be a mess. With good notebooks now available at the 1000 dollar level, we had thought more students would use their own computer rather than those supplied in the library. But that evolution is taking much longer than I had anticipated. Every time we discuss reducing the number of computers we get a lot of protests."

WORKSTATIONS

The Library offers 48 fully functional workstations for patrons, fewer than most major research libraries, but keep in mind the limited base of undergraduates, only about one thousand. These workstations are loaded with an array of applications software, as well as catalog, database and internet access. As mentioned, the Library also offers 15 laptops on library loan, as well as 12 quick access workstations. These instant access stations will soon be phased out to be replaced by fully functional workstations. Their capabilities are currently restricted to access to the Library website, the catalog and a limited range of databases. Explains Vandevelde, "The idea is that most of the workstations are always busy so there should be some on which you can just look up a book. The truth is that the intent was good (in implementing the restricted workstations) but when you look at the usage it is really so low that you question if they are of any use at all."

URL RESOLVER

The Library uses SFX. "We were the first academic library to use it, in March 2001," notes Vandevelde.

WEBSITE

The website is managed collaboratively by two librarians and two technology specialists from the IT Department. Currently, the site is shifting from Microsoft to Linux.

The Library offers request forms from the library web page that allows for requests from the shelves of closed archives. Recently, the Library jettisoned its home grown room reservation system in favor of an open source solution.

VIRTUAL REFERENCE

The Library does not have a virtual reference system. Explains Vandevelde-"It is one of these things where I - the IT person - I am more interested than the reference librarians. The reference librarians are not particularly interested; they see it as too impersonal."

SOFTWARE FOR ELECTRONIC COLLECTION

Currently, the Library does not use any proprietary software to track its digital collection but Vandevelde notes: "Our cataloging librarian has been requesting that we buy it; it is definitely on the wish list of the cataloger."

ADVICE

"My main source of information is the Coalition for Networked Information. Basically in two days for every six months I get so much information distilled."

SALT LAKE COMMUNITY COLLEGE

DESCRIPTION OF SALT LAKE COMMMUNITY COLLEGE

Salt Lake Community College is a large community college with an FTE enrollment of 14,325 students. The College has a main library and smaller libraries at four other locations. We spoke with Eloise Vanderhooft, Director of Technical Services, Salt Lake Community College.

WORKSTATIONS

The Library offers about 100 patron-accessible workstations including those in a student computer lab that is run by the college IT department; the main library offers 12 workstations for student access. The Library has no plans to add additional workstations; most of the current workstations are from Dell.

SIZE & COMPOSITION OF THE IT DEPARTMENT

The IT staff has 3 full time and 2 part time employees. Two people work largely on issues involved with networking, workstations and related equipment and the online catalog.

Last year, the Library had 12.07 student assistants FTE – (all libraries) but only 2 full time people working on IT systems and the department had no student help.

ONLINE CATALG

The library's online catalog is Dynix which has a major statewide contract in Utah that includes most academic and public libraries. The Utah state legislature wanted all of the libraries under state auspices to be on the same system. Only Brigham Young, the largest university in the State, is on a different system, as Vanderhooft explains: "Since the University could not wait for the group to make a decision, we did an RFP and all the libraries went in together. It was more a consensus approach. There are different modules that you look at. We had to have input from all of the libraries. It was a very long and work intensive project; it took a lot before we could decide. However, I would say we are pretty satisfied with Dynix. Copy cataloging is outsourced to OCLC and we are looking into outsourcing all cataloging – to PromptCat. (When it comes to the catalog and cataloging) Mostly it is time; we do not have the staff so our main concern is staff time."

WEB SITE

The web site is run out of the IT Department. One person spends much of her time running the ILS system – Horizon, - and the library web site.

DATABASES

The Library offers access to a broad range of databases through the Utah academic consortium. Many Ebsco databases are offered through this consortium. Salt Lake Community College students can also link to an interface through which they can search all of the academic libraries in the state at once.

URL RESOLVER

"We don't have anything like serials solutions – we can't afford it right now. We could go through the University of Utah – but that would be one more step for the patrons. If I click on their electronic journals and if it is indexed in one of the databases that our consortiums have in common, then I can go right to that journal . I can log into the University of Utah's Catalog."

WISH LIST

"We have databases we are looking at all the time. There are numerous ones we do look at. We do a lot of trials but we can't always afford them. The systems people have a wish list, believe me."

VIRTUAL REFERENCE

We belong to a nationwide group called 24x7, live chat. We have been on it for a year or more. Our reference people like it and we take turns (contributing time to man the service.)

WIRELESS ACCESS

"We have it throughout the campus; we have had it now for about two years. At first it was very difficult to get it to work. It was slow because there were not enough boxes. The problem was if there were too many people on it, it would be very very slow. We got in when it was very leading edge but as far as I know it is working."

COMPUTER LAB

"A lot of people come in for the computer lab. It get them in the library and they can use it do their papers. We have had it for five or six years. It is managed by the IT group but they work closely with us and any problems that come up we resolve them together."

TECHNOLOGY TRAINING FOR STUDENTS

We have a lab in the library that we can train. There are ten computers in a classroom in the main library. When other campus libraries need it we can teach the course in other labs. We can give very general classes or work with faculty members for subject specific classes. Last year we had 172 presentations and that covered 2,393 students. Each presentation generally lasts about 50 minutes."

HUTCHINSON COMMUNITY COLLEGE AND AREA VOCATIONAL SCHOOL

DESCRIPTION OF THE HUTCHINSON COMMUNITY COLLEGE AND AREA VOCATIONAL SCHOOL

Hutchinson Area Community College and Area Vocational School is a fast growing community college with about 1900 full time students and more than 3000 part time students. The College has specialized programs in fire management and healthcare information systems, and has a large and well established distance learning program. The library has 5.5 FTE positions and 1.5 FTE positions for student helpers. In addition to a main library site, the library maintains two smaller sites at outlying campuses.

We spoke with Mr. Robert Kelly, Coordinator of Library Services for Hutchinson.

WORKSTATIONS

The Library itself has 15 workstations for patron access which are equipped with the Microsoft Office suite, internet and catalog access, and some course specific software when applicable. The Library is housed in the basement of a building it shares with an entity called The Rimmer Learning Resource Center, and this Center has 70 workstations. The Library has a separate budget but in many senses is actually a component of the

Resource Center, itself a formidable undertaking that offers extensive tutoring for students, among other services.

"What they primarily do up there is tutoring and student support services so they have tutors - both student and non-student tutors and there is a significant amount of grant funding that goes to that program," explains Kelly. "Any student who attends here can get tutoring assistance. The resource center has a writing lab and a math lab staffed by tutors." The Learning Resource Center is open until one in the morning give nights per week and, though the Library tries to complement its efforts and be available to its patrons, it does not follow the same punishing schedule. Anywhere from 5 to 25 students are in the tutoring center at any one time, and the Center has a staff of more than 20 tutors.

The physical proximity of the tutoring services, and the tendency of the tutors to help their students exploit the Library, has influenced the Library's mission by encouraging it to informally cooperate with the tutoring service. Although the Library has no formal information literacy requirements for students, Kelly feels that aggressive outreach to faculty and students, and cooperation with the tutors and students of the tutoring Center has led to significant increases in overall use of the Library and vastly increased familiarity with its resources. Hutchinson's experience is similar to many other colleges in that the idea of "taking the library to the student," as much as the other way around, has led to significant increases information literacy among populations that might not otherwise have acquired these skills. In Kelly's view, exposure and encouragement are half the battle. Kelly emphasizes the importance of personalization, for both faculty and students, in showing them just which library databases and information resources impact their field of study and future prospects.

DATABASES

The Library offers a suite of databases that are available to all Kansas residents, as well as those licensed by the State of Kansas specifically for college students under the auspices of the Regents Library Database Consortium (RLDC). The Library also licenses databases on its own but most are through the Consortium. The College grants to distance learning students access to its databases through *WebCT*. Kelly is also developing a tutorial that he feels will be especially beneficial to the distance ed students.

NEW LIBRARY SITE

Hutchinson opened the new joint library/learning resource center building in 2003. Kelly notes that the combining of the two entities, as well as the availability of new library resources and an aggressive and personalized marketing effort, led to a big increase in library use. Despite the increase in electronic offerings students used print books more This is a common in community colleges, as better electronic info resources draw more students into the library and the use of all library resources increases, even paper-based resources.

"Last year book use was the highest it has been in three years," says Kelly, who adds: "The impact on the tutoring services and the resources and the availability of the Library -- a retooling of our instruction program has made a vast difference as well. Previously instruction was too complicated and the instructors in classes - they did not like bringing their classes over because they did not find it useful. We changed a lot of things. Initially it is getting the students in the building and then it is building on that. It is making it meaningful for them."

Both aggressive outreach and careful consideration to the geographic proximity of library resources have spurred usage:

"The Library and the Learning Resource center had been separate and our distance education staff was spread around campus; the re-organization enabled the distance ed people and the student services to find a home," says Kelly.

FIVE FACTORS IN BETTER TECHNOLOGY TRAINING

Kelly emphasizes that better student training in use of a library's resources leads to more and more satisfying use of those resources. One trick is to make sure that instruction is interactive, particularly initial instruction designed to catch interest. "The breadth and quality of instruction is better if it is much more interactive. With the general orientation

Exercise I have a match exercise and they have to compare the list of items and they have to find them in the library. And we don't just show them the workstations. We have a 15 workstation lab in the library and we walk them through it -- it is part of the orientation class. Also, instructors make library familiarity a for-credit assignment within the context of their classes."

Mr. Kelly recommends aggressive and personalized outreach, stressing that a librarian needs to spend some time out of the library attending faculty and departmental meetings, meeting with department heads and showing up at special events.

WEB SITE MANAGEMENT

"The Library web site is housed on the College's server and a library staff member updates our web page; there is also a campus webmaster."

HELP DESK

A help desk is manned by the College IT Department.

DIGITAL REFERENCE

The Library has decided not to take part in the statewide online reference services - Ask Kansas.

ELECTRONIC BOOKS

The Library provides access to several collections from *NetLibrary* through a link on its web site. The Library also links the full text of *NetLibrary* titles directly to its online catalog, enabling click through access to text directly from the catalog. There are sets that are made available by *NetLibary* through the Bibliographic Center for Research - -based in Denver -- a regional consortium.

Ebook use is increasing rapidly. According to Kelly "the Ebooks are used very heavily. Use is going crazy. .Medically- related books are used quite a bit some things in the social sciences, especially topically related materials are also heavily used. Some of our legal materials, for example, a legal dictionary that is used far more than any other item which tells me our paralegals are using it quite a bit, the distance ed students are using it quite a bit."

Kelly has become a convert to the importance of Ebooks in the community college collection.

"I had been a skeptic about them but when it comes to supporting distance ed students, you need to consider them. Also if you have a commuter based campus, or if you have space limitations it is something to consider. So, there are a lot of reasons to consider electronic books."

HUTCHINSON'S TOP TEN EBOOKTITLES

JULY 1, 2003-- JUNE 30 -- 2004

Number of accesses in brackets

Bi-Polar Disorders: A Guide to Helping Children and Adolescents -- (10)

No Higher Court: Contemporary Feminism and the Right to Abortion --(9)

Cliffs Test Prep ACT (college entrance exam)-- (9)

How To Do Everything with HTML -- (8)

Transformative Motherhood: On Giving and Getting in a Consumer Culture -- (8)

Understanding Childhood Obesity -- (7)

Parenting a Child with Diabetes -- (7)

SAM's Teach Yourself PC Upgrades in 10 Minutes (6)

The Rabbit on the Face of the Moon: Mythology in the Mezoamerican Tradition-6

Marijuana & Medicine --6

Kelly believes that computer books make ideal Ebook investments. "I definitely do a lot of comparing of what we have online with what we have in our collection," he explains.

"A good instance is computer books. Shelf life doesn't last long and the computer books online get good use."

ADVICE

"One of the very first lessons that I learned as a librarian is that you need to identify who your core users are. Even if you are not there, your best marketing is faculty word of mouth. If you take care of your core users they will tell everyone everything that they are doing. You need to know who your core is and build your services around your core and build it from there. I have worked in five different school districts and two college libraries and that philosophy has worked for me every single time. And, really you have to get out of the office - marketing, marketing, marketing, find out what people need."

MONASH UNIVERSITY

GENERAL DESCRIPTION OF MONASH UNIVERSITY

Monash University, headquartered in Melbourne, Victoria, is one of Australia's largest research universities, perhaps best known for its programs in the biomedical sciences and business administration. Monash is a national institution funded by the Australian federal government; it has 35,000 FTE students. Monash has a main campus and four smaller campuses in the general Mebourne area, another in Gippsland which is also in Victoria about 150 miles from Melbourne, as well as two overseas campuses, one in Malaysia and another in South Africa.

The library administration is centralized in the main Melbourne campus and virtually all functions for the Melbourne campuses, and some functions for the library buildings of the other campuses, are handled from the main Melbourne campus. The Library controls 10 buildings, of which three are on the main campus, one each on the other four Melbourne-area campuses, and one each in the Gippsland, Malaysian and South African campuses. The main library administration in Melbourne negotiates virtually all database licenses for the campuses, including the overseas campuses, and supports all enterprise-wide information systems. However, the main Melbourne library administration does not have IT staff at the overseas campuses. The Main University IT department does, however, and the main library staff interfaces with the University-IT staff in the overseas campuses to coordinate library-related IT decision making with these campuses.

The overall centralized library budget is approximately $20 million; the Library IT staff budget, approximately $2 million. We spoke with Mr. Simon Huggard, Systems Manager for the Monash University Library.

DATABASE LICENSING

Database licensing is centralized for all of the campuses. According to Huggard, the percentage of licensing done through consortia "is probably about 50 percent" and "the consortiums are mostly with other government universities and other institutions such as the Defense Force Academy. The main consortium deals are done through the Council of Australian University Librarians which is mostly restricted to libraries from Australia plus a few from New Zealand."

The Library has sometimes had trouble in adding its Malaysian and South African campuses to its database licenses, since vendors have sometimes balked at adding campuses from far flung countries. Thee vendors consider this poaching on the distributors that they may already have in these markets. "So we have occasionally had to compromise in this respect," says Huggard.

INFORMATION LITERACY

Although the University has no official information literacy requirement, it has "quite an active program, according to Huggard, and "there has been a big push to have information literacy incorporated into many courses." The library has a librarian devoted full time to info literacy issues and courses in the law and engineering schools have been configured with specific information literacy goals in mind."

IT STAFF

The library has an IT staff of 15, including those who spend much of their time visiting the branch campuses. The overseas libraries have some separate staff of their own. The unit's service support group has 6 FTE employees, all IT professionals with a qualifying post graduate degree or certificate in an IT discipline. This staff largely services the desktop pc's, handles the printers and photocopiers, and attends to the servers that the library controls directly.

PRINTING TECHNOLOGY

The Library charges students 10 cents (Australian) per page and students get no allotment of free print outs; the library patrons print out an average of roughly 500,000 pages per month; annual revenues are more than a half million dollars.

WORKSTATIONS

The library inventory of deployed pc's, which are on a three year replacement cycle, is approximately 1000, and they are mostly HP Compaq and IBM.

"We stopped using IBM about a year ago," says Huggard, "the University made a different agreement. We found that local service contracts from IBM were not very good they were not good at fixing problems."

Most workstations have Windows 2000 or windows XP, as well as web browsers. Some offer access only to the internet, the library OPAC and library supplied databases while about 200 are fully equipped with Microsoft Office. Eventually the Library would like to supply most of the OPAC access computers with applications software as well.

VIRTUAL REFERENCE

"We have the LSSI product which is really good. We chose that one because it did not require any particular PC software to download and it uses standard web browsers. It does not get hugely used, but people appreciate it when they use it, and it supports co-browsing."

WIRELESS ACCESS

The Library began to offer wireless access about three years ago and initially it was scantly used. Now, however, it is much more heavily used, particularly in the legal and medical libraries. The Library has plans to extend wireless access to more and more buildings.

WEB SITE

The IT division manages the entire library web site. IT sets up templates and helps manage the content management system although the library web site runs off of the university servers and not those controlled directly by the library. Recently, by agreement with the major in-house content providers to the web site, the IT staff and the content providers (mostly subject specific or task specific librarians) changed the system to approve web site changes.

Approvals used to be routed through the IT staff "but they would get 100 emails per day," says Huggard, "So, now the approval goes from those who edit the content to their own director and it is all done online. We use Interwoven as a content management system."

The IT division has two full time staff devoted to running the web site, a director or webmaster and an assistant, both of whom are librarians.

SEARCH FROM THE WEBSITE

The Library is using an Infoseek search engine for its website but "a lot of committees are looking at Metadata and a whole lot of other things," notes Huggard.

URL RESOLVER

The Library uses SFX but also has made a large independent effort over several years to provide URL links that go directly to full text documents, mostly in PDF.

"We have something like 90,000 urls's that go directly to full text content at the journal and article level," explains Huggard, who continues: "There is a mixture of things that we have done We have done a lot of work to get a list of URL's and put them into our catalog and we have done some local programming and have been getting library vendors to create URL's that go directly to the content. The more we publicize (the links to electronic content from the catalog) the more usage goes through the roof."

EBOOKS

Huggard says that Ebook usage is "huge". "We have bought the *Safari Ebooks*, *NetLibrary*, *Books24x7*. We have in the range of 15,000 Ebooks.

"We still buy a lot of print books for undergraduate courses but it does influence in terms of numbers of multiple copies of print books that we buy. We try to get the Ebooks so we can eliminate as much as possible multiple (print) copies."

ELECTRONIC COURSE RESERVE

The Library is trying to save time and money by creating web pages "which are electronic reading lists which are directly tailored for each course. We have direct links into catalogs and we create direct links to the PDF's." The system creates a historic record of the types of electronic resources required for different courses and instructors. Each new semester the links can be updated as needed, but much of the repetitive work involved in electronic course reserve administration can be eliminated. "And we can do it all from the Library website," says Huggard happily. "And if we don't have an electronic version to link to, we can link to a print copy in the catalog and that will signal that the book should be put on course reserve."

DIGITIZATION OF SPECIAL COLLECTIONS

The Library is just starting to digitize its special collections. The Library's Gippland facility has a special collection of 4000 photographic images of Victoria Province that will be digitized next year. The University's teaching hospital will digitize a series of X-Ray images that will be useful for teaching purposes, and a specialized collection of Jewish music will also be digitized in the very near future, as will a collection of art images.

Although the library does not have a major digital library initiative, Huggard points out that Monash has been scanning chapter and books into databases and putting them up on the internet for many years.

Australian universities reached an agreement with many Australian publishers to develop a licensing system similar to the one in place in the United States for photocopying through the Copyright Clearance Center. "We used to write to every single publisher to ask permission to scan their works, and some required us to pay a fee. But the COPYRIGHT AGENCY LIMITED made an agreement with the Australian Vice Chancellor's Committee – AVCC and it covers all of the Australian universities. We can use the works of whomever is registered with this agency – both books and journals. We pay a license fee per number of students enrolled, something like $5.00 per student, or something like. It has an audit component and reporting component (that requires some record keeping).

FOR THE FUTURE

The Library is looking into improving its disaster recovery services, and better enabling fall over from one server to another when one server gets into trouble. It is also looking into better means of image updating its PC's, anything that will decrease the labor time demands of this maintenance. Other topics of interest are automating electronic collection management and furthering the cause of linking catalog entries to full text.

OTHER REPORTS FROM PRIMARY RESEARCH GROUP INC.

BEST PRACTICES OF PUBLIC LIBRARY INFORMATION TECHNOLOGY DIRECTORS
Price: $65.00   Publication Date: February 2005   ISBN: 1-57440-073-8

This special report from Primary Research Group is based on exhaustive interviews with information technology directors and other critical staff involved in IT decision-making from The Princeton Public Library, the Minneapolis Public Library, the Boston Public Library, the Seattle Public Library, Cedar Rapids Public Library, San Francisco Public Library, the Denver Public Library, Evansville Public Library and the Santa Monica Public Library. The report – which is in an interview format and presents the views of the institutions cited above as well as Primary Research Group commentary – presents insights into the myriad of technology related issues confronting today's public librarians, including issues involved with: internet filtering, workstation management and development, pc image roll out, equipment and vendor selection, database licensing, internet access policies, automated book check in and check out systems, cataloging, and catalog enhancement, voice over IP, digitization of special collections, development of technology centers, wireless access, use of ebooks, outsourcing, IT staff training, virtual reference, and much more.

TRAINING COLLEGE STUDENTS IN INFORMATION LITERACY: PROFILES OF HOW COLLEGES TEACH THEIR STUDENTS TO USE ACADEMIC LIBRARIES
ISBN#: 1-57440-059-2   Publication Date: January 2003   Price: $69.50
This special report profiles how more than a dozen academic libraries are coping with the surge of web/database education requests. The report covers the development of online tutorials, distribution of teaching loads and levels of specialization among library staff, the perils of teaching library science to English 101 and Psychology 101 students, as well as advanced personalized tutorials for PHD candidates and professors.   Among the specialized topics covered: how libraries are reaching out and teaching distance learners, how are they negotiating help from other college departments such as academic computing and education and from in-house instructional technology programmers. Other issues explored include the library education efforts of consortiums and partnerships, use of knowledge management and reference software for library training, the development of savvy library web pages and tutorials for training, and the thorny issue of negotiating training support from vendors.

CREATING THE VIRTUAL REFERENCE SERVICE
ISBN 1-57440-058-4   PRICE: $85.00   PUBLICATION DATE: January 18, 2003
This report profiles the efforts of 15 academic, special and public libraries to develop digital reference services. The aim of the study is to enable other libraries to benefit from their experience in deciding whether and how to develop a digital reference service, how much time, money and other resources to spend on it, how to plan it, institute it and evaluate it. Let librarians - in their own words - tell you about their experiences with digital reference.

Among the libraries and other organizations profiled are: Pennsylvania State University, Syracuse University's Virtual Reference Desk, the Massachusetts Institute of Technology, Palomar College, The Library of Congress, the University of Florida, PA Librarian Live, the Douglas County Public Library, the

Cleveland Public Library, Denver Public Library, OCLC, the New England Law Library Consortium, the Internet Public Library, Paradise Valley Community College, Yale University Law School, Oklahoma State University, Tutor.Com and Baruch College.

PRIVATE COLLEGE INFORMATION TECHNOLOGY BENCHMARKS
ISBN: 1-57440-060-6   PRICE: $295.00   Publication Date: January 20, 2003
Private College Information Technology Benchmarks presents more than 650 tables and charts exploring the use of information technology by small and medium sized private college in the United States. The report covers both academic and administrative computing, and breaks out data by enrollment size and level of tuition charged. Sixteen private American colleges contributed data to the report.

LAW LIBRARY BENCHMARKS, 2004-05 EDITION
Expected Publication Date: August 20004   Price: $115.00   ISBN #: 1-57440-070-3
Law Library Benchmarks presents data from more than 70 law libraries, including those of major law firms, law schools, government agencies and courthouses. Data is broken out by type of law library. Includes detailed data on: library dimensions and physical and "e-traffic" to the library, trends in library staff size, salaries and budget, precise statistics on use of librarian time, spending trends in the library content budget, spending on specific types of legal information such as state and local codes or legal journals, spending on databases and commercial online services, use of and plans for CD-ROM, parent organization management's view of the future of the law library, assessment of library resources for analyzing the business side of law, assessment of attorney search skills, trends in use of reference materials and much more.

BEST PRACTICES OF PUBLIC LIBRARY INFORMATION TECHNOLOGY DIRECTORS
Price: $65.00   Publication Date: February 2005   ISBN: 1-57440-073-8
This special report is based on exhaustive interviews with information technology directors and other critical staff involved in IT decision-making from public libraries of Princeton, Evansville, San Francisco, Boston, Denver, Santa Monica, Columbus, Minneapolis, Cedar Falls and Seattle. The report – which is in an interview format and presents the views of the institutions cited above as well as Primary Research Group commentary – presents insights into the myriad of technology related issues confronting today's public librarians, including issues involved with: technology department staffing, internet filtering, workstation management and development, equipment and vendor selection, database licensing, internet access policies, automated book check in and check out systems, data back up, web site maintenance, cataloging, catalog enhancements, digitization of special collections, development of wireless access and other issues of interest to public librarians.

THE SURVEY OF ACADEMIC LIBRARIES, 2004 EDITION
Price: $80.00   ISBN #: 1-57440-067-3   Publication Date: March 28, 2004
This new report is based on a detailed survey of academic libraries, focusing on their acquisition and budget & expenditure policies. Includes data on current and planned purchases of information in print formats and electronic formats and explores planned trade-offs between the two. Also gives precise data on spending on books, Ebooks, databases, CD-ROM, journals and other information vehicles. Breaks down electronic information spending into three categories: from aggregators, from publishers directly by subscription, from publishers, non subscription. Also presents detailed data on use of documents delivery services, articles "pulled down" from publisher web sites, use of subscription agents, trends in information literacy training, use of virtual reference services, extent of library web site evaluations, and trends in librarian hiring and salaries. Also examines the perceived attitudes of college administrations towards the library and charts plans for library expansion/contraction.

LICENSING AND COPYRIGHT MANAGEMENT: BEST PRACTICES OF COLLEGE, SPECIAL AND RESEARCH LIBRARIES

Price: $80.00   ISBN# 1-57440-068-1   Publication Date: May 2004

This report looks closely at the licensing and copyright management strategies of a sample of leading research, college and special libraries and consortiums and includes interviews with leading experts. The focus is on electronic database licensing, and includes discussions of the most pressing issues: development of consortiums and group buying initiatives, terms of access, liability for infringement, archiving, training and development, free trial periods, contract language, contract management software and time management issues, acquiring and using usage statistics, elimination of duplication, enhancement of bargaining power, open access publishing policies, interruption of service contingency arrangements, changes in pricing over the life of the contract, interlibrary loan of electronic files, copyright clearance, negotiating tactics, uses of consortiums -- and many other issues. The report profiles the emergence of consortiums and group buying arrangements.

CREATING THE DIGITAL ACADEMIC LIBRARY:

Price: $69.50   Publication Date: July 15, 2004   ISBN #: 1-57440- 071-1

This report looks closely at the efforts of more than ten major academic libraries to develop their digital assets and deal with problems in the area of librarian time management, database selection, vendor relations, contract negotiation and tracking, electronic resources funding and marketing, technical development, archival access, open access publishing agit prop, use of ebooks, digitization of audio and image collections and other areas of the development of the digital academic library. Includes profiles of Columbia University School of Medicine, The Health Sciences Complex of the University of Texas, Duke University Law Library, The University of Indiana Law Library, The University of South Carolina, the University of Idaho and many others.